SECRET KITCHEN

AN ARGENTINE COOKING BOOK

TAMMY CREO

PublishAmerica
Baltimore

First printing

At the specific preference of the author, PublishAmerica allowed this work to remain exactly as the author intended, verbatim, without editorial input.

ISBN: 1-4241-6629-2
PUBLISHED BY PUBLISHAMERICA, LLLP
www.publishamerica.com
Baltimore

Printed in the United States of America

Dedication

To my mother Fresia Millaron,
And her passion for cooking.

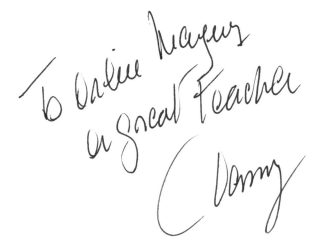

To Darlene Maguy
a great Teacher
Danny

Acknowledgments

I want to thank my daughter Barbara for her encouragement, support and her time helping me with my manuscript.

To Liam and Katie because they bring love, joy, and inspiration to my life.

And to my mother, who in life, always encouraged me, and still does…

From Buenos Aires to Georgia,
Mouth-watering recipes, unfamiliar to most!

Impress your friends and family with new easy recipes!
For vegetarians too!
Make fresh home-made pasta like an Italian
Be admired, envied, and loved with these new dishes!

The best combination of European and Argentinean
traditions mixed together to offer the most delicious recipes!

INTRODUCTION

For those who are unfamiliar with the Argentinean cuisine, I would like to summarize by saying that Argentina is a land of immigrants. The majority of its population is comprised of people of Spanish and Italian ancestry. In the late nineteenth and early twentieth centuries, Argentina experienced a flood of European immigration from many different parts of Europe. With only a three percent native Indian or mestizo population, the current Argentinean population is primarily European. Due to the legacy of cultural diversity, one will find dishes from the best Spanish, Italian, French, and German cuisine, with additional flavors originated by the native cooking. The combination of European and Folklore traditions gives the Argentine cuisine a very unique mix of flavors.

The recipes contained in this book include typical home-style dishes, as well as, some of the most exquisite recipes that you can find at the finest restaurants in Buenos Aires. While Argentina's meat dishes are most popular, and probably most familiar to tourists in Buenos Aires, there is a wide range of delicious recipes served in Argentine households that are completely unfamiliar to most and yet are quite delectable!

CONTENTS

Cakes and Desserts

BASIC PASTA

INGREDIENTS

Three Cups of Durum Wheat
(Option: Replace one Cup of Durum Wheat with Flour)
One Teaspoon of Salt
Three Eggs
One Tablespoon of Olive Oil
Salt and Pepper.

Mix the durum wheat and salt together. Form a mound with the durum wheat and create a well in the center of the mound. Beat the eggs and oil together in a bowl, and then pour this mixture into the well.

Mix well the durum wheat and eggs, working from the outside until the flour and eggs are mixed. Start kneading the dough with both hands. Let it rest for twenty minutes in the refrigerator. Then remove from refrigerator and let it temper for 10 minutes. Flour a surface, and work the dough on it. Roll out the dough to half inch thick and cut into pieces, and using a pasta machine work one piece at the time. Place the pasta carefully sprinkled with flour to prevent from sticking.

Bring a pot of water to boil, add salt and a little bit of oil, cook for about five minutes, or until the pasta is risen and tender. Drain and toss the pasta on a dish to serve with oil, salt and pepper or your favorite sauce.

TOMATO SAUCE

INGREDIENTS

Three Medium Chopped Onions
Minced Garlic
Chopped Parsley
One Can of Tomato Paste
Two Cups of Water
Oregano
Salt
Pepper
Olive Oil

In a saucepan sauté the onion and garlic. Add the parsley and seasoning, when onions are transparent. Add the tomato paste and water. Let it cook slow for fifteen minutes.

Serve on top of pasta with grated parmesan cheese.

LASAGNA

INGREDIENTS

One Can of Tomato Sauce
One Lb. of Ground Beef (Sautéed with onions (or Vegetarian Ground Beef or Tofu) (See resources for vegetarian at the end of the book)
One Cup and a Half of Ricotta Cheese
One Cup of Parmesan Cheese
Four or Five Cloves of Garlic (Crushed)
Chopped Parsley
Sliced Red or Green Peppers
Two Cups and a Half of Mozzarella Cheese
Salt, Pepper, Oregano and Olive Oil

Make the "Basic Pasta" dough (see recipe), then put it on a table and knead it with a rolling pin, making a thin layer, and the size of the baking pan you are going to use. Make about three layers.

Spread a little tomato sauce evenly on the bottom of the pan and olive oil, and place the first layer. Top this layer with ricotta cheese and parmesan and put the second layer on top. Cover this one with the tomato sauce, ground beef previously sauté with onions (you can use veggie meat) crushed garlic, oregano, salt and pepper, cover with the third layer. Spread a little tomato sauce all over, add crushed garlic, parsley, sliced peppers, or any vegetable you like, cover with one cup of parmesan cheese and two cups and a half of mozzarella.

Bake in the oven at 350 degrees for about thirty five to forty minutes or until the cheese is bubbling.

RAVIOLI

Make the "Basic Pasta", spread with a rolling pin, and make two layers. Using a Ravioli maker, cut a sheet of pasta dough into two rectangles, each slightly larger than the ravioli plates. Sprinkle the top of the metal plate and the bottom of the plastic plate with flour, and put one rectangle of dough over the plate and gently press the plastic plate into it to stretch the dough and form pockets. Remove the top plate, fill the pockets with the filling, and then, moisten the dough along the lines before topping it with the other rectangle of dough, then with a rolling pin back and forth over the dough until all the ravioli are cut and sealed, then tap on the table to release the pasta.

Filling:

Mix one cup of Ricotta cheese, half cup of blue cheese, half cup of Brie, half cup of Parmesan, one crushed garlic, pepper, salt and half a cup of heavy cream, and one egg all together in a blender.

CANELONI A LA ROSSINI

INGREDIENTS

Flour 350 grams. (Can be combined with semolina)
Two Eggs
Salt and Water

FILLING INGREDIENTS

White Sauce
One Chopped Onion
Olive Oil
Ham (cut into pieces)
Devil Ham
One cup of Parmesan Cheese
Pate de Foe
Salt, Pepper, Nutmeg

Note: Meats can be replaced by vegetarian Meat or Tofu. See last page of book for more information.

Place the flour on a flat surface, make a well and add the eggs in the center, the water and salt and make soft dough. Knead the dough, then spread very thin, and cut into squares of about three to four inches. Boil the pasta for five minutes in hot water and then place them over a flat surface and sprinkle with Parmesan cheese.

Note: if you use semolina with flour, you don't need to boil the pasta.

~CONTINUED~

FILLING

Fry the onion and then put it in a bowl and add the white sauce, the ham, devil ham, pate, the eggs, the parmesan cheese, salt, pepper and nutmeg. Mix all the ingredients well. Then fill the squares with this filling, roll them, and place them on a baking dish and cover them with the white sauce, and parmesan cheese and bake at 300 degree for about 15 minutes.

GNOCCHI

INGREDIENTS

Five Medium Potatoes
Two Eggs
Two Cups of Flour
Half a Bunch of Parsley
Salt and Pepper
Butter
Milk
Salt

Peel the potatoes and cut them in pieces. Boil water and add the potatoes and salt. When the potatoes are cooked, drain them, and make mash potatoes adding the milk and the butter. Once you have your mash potato, add the eggs and the parsley and enough flour to give it consistency and place this mix on a surface previously sprinkled with flour to avoid sticking.

Work the dough well, add more flour as needed, and form a ball. Cut the ball into four pieces. Take a piece and knead it and make a rope, about one inch thick. With a knife cut it into small pieces about one inch long. Using a fork place each gnocchi and roll it over the fork to shape it. Cook the gnocchi in boiling water and salt for about five minutes. They will rise to the surface when done.

Drain the gnocchi, place them on a dish and cover them with tomato sauce, white sauce, or your favorite sauce, add parmesan cheese on top.

MEAT EMPANADAS

DOUGH INGREDIENTS

14 Ounces of Flour
Eight Ounces of Butter
One Cup of Cold Water
One Teaspoon of Lemon Juice
Salt

In a bowl, mix the flour, salt, butter and add the lemon juice and water slowly, and alternating both. After this is all well mixed, put it on the table and work the dough with both hands and then stretch with the rolling pin. Fold the dough in four and let it rest for one hour.

Stretch the dough well with the rolling pin, and cut into 12 inches or 14 inches round shapes.

FILLING

Three Medium Yellow Onions - Chopped
Hamburger Meat (Veggie Ground Beef optional) Three Cups
1/4 Cup of Olives
1/2 Cup of Seedless Raisin
Six Hard Boiled Eggs
Oregano - Cumin - Pepper - Salt

~CONTINUED~

In a frying pan, fry the chopped onions until tender, add the meat, the oregano, cumin, pepper and salt. Let it cook well for about ten minutes. Add the olives and raisins and let it cook in a low heat for another ten minutes. In a bowl mix all the cooked ingredients with the hard boiled eggs cut into pieces.

Place about two spoonful of the mix in the center of the round dough and fold the disk, bringing the edges together and then push to borders to lock in the ingredients. You can also decorate the borders by pressing all around with a fork. Brush them on top with an egg.

Place the empanadas in a buttered pan and bake for about 25 minutes at 375 degrees. They can also be fried instead of baked for crispier taste.

CHEESE EMPANADAS

DOUGH INGREDIENTS

14 Ounces of Flour
Eight Ounces of Butter
One Third Cup of Cold Water
One Teaspoon of Lemon Juice
Salt

In a bowl, mix the flour, salt, butter and add the lemon juice and water slowly, and alternating both. After this is all well mixed, put it on the table and work the dough with both hands and then stretch with the rolling pin. Fold the dough in four and let it rest for one hour.

Stretch the dough well with the rolling pin, and cut into 12 inches or 14 inches round shapes.

FILLING

Swiss Cheese - Mozzarella Cheese
Oregano - Pepper - Salt

Mix all ingredients together and fill the empanadas. Bake or fry.

CORN EMPANADAS

Same procedure except for the filling.

FILLING

Sautéed Chopped Onions
Crashed Garlic
A Can of Sweet Corn

Mix all ingredients and add hard boiled eggs cut in small pieces. Fill the empanadas with this filling. Bake or fry.

PIZZA

INGREDIENTS

Flour One Lb.
Yeast One ounce
Half Cup of Warm Water
Salt and Sugar
One Cup of Olive Oil

TOPPINGS

Tomato Paste One can
Crushed Red Pepper
Oregano
Salt
Three Cups of Mozzarella Cheese

In a bowl mix the flour with the yeast dissolved in warm water with a little of sugar, add the salt, the oil, and let it rest for 10 minutes at room temperature. Let it rise. Knead the dough well to make it soft and stretch it on to a pizza pan previously greased. Let it rest another 10 minutes and then add the toppings. Bake in oven at 400 degrees for about 15 to 20 minutes.

FAINA

INGREDIENTS

One full cup of Chick-pea Flour
Two Cups of Water
Three Spoonfuls of Oil
Salt and Pepper

In a bowl put the flour with the water, oil, salt and pepper, mix and let it rest all night. Then add more water as needed to make a soft, creamy mix. Grease a pizza pan and pour the mix in it, add oil on top and bake at 375 degrees for about 10 to 15 minutes.

POTATO PIE

INGREDIENTS

Ten Medium Potatoes
One Stick of Butter
Half a Cup of Heavy Cream
One Cup of Mozzarella Cheese
Six Hard Boiled Eggs
Half Lb. of Ground Beef (You can use Vegetarian Ground Beef)
Two Large Chopped Onions
Parsley
Olive Oil - Salt and Pepper
Cumin
One Bell Pepper Cut in small pieces
One Jar of Olives
One cup and a half of Raisin

In a frying pan sauté the chopped onions in olive oil, add parsley, bell pepper, ground beef, salt, pepper and cumin. After 15 minutes add the hard boiled eggs cut into pieces, the olives and the raisins and let it simmer for five minutes.

Boil the potatoes with salt, and when cooked, make soft mashed potatoes mixing the cream and butter.

In a large oven dish, spread one layer of mash potatoes, using half of the prepared mashed potatoes. Add the mix with ground beef already prepared and spread evenly. Cover with the rest of the mash potatoes and top it with mozzarella cheese. Bake in the oven for about twenty minutes at 375 degrees. Serve hot.

SPANISH EMPANADA

INGREDIENTS

Two Cups of Flour
A Pinch of Salt
One Teaspoon of Sugar
Yeast
Half a Cup of Warm Water

FILLING

Two Cans of Tuna
Three Medium Size Onions
Six Hard Boiled Eggs
One Egg
Bell Red Pepper
Olives
Olive oil
Parsley
Cumin
Salt and pepper

With the flour make a well and stir in the yeast dissolved in the water with sugar, add the salt. Now knead the dough until it is smooth, and let it rest in a warm place for half an hour.

In a frying pan, sauté the onions with olive oil, add parsley, bell pepper, Cumin, salt and pepper. Add the tuna, olives and the eggs.

~CONTINUED~

In a greased baking pan spread half the dough evenly and pour the filling. Cover with the rest of the dough and press together around the edges, and brush the top with a beaten egg to give it shine. Bake for about 30 minutes at 375 degrees.

PASCUALINA PIE

INGREDIENTS

Filo Dough
Two Lbs. of Spinach
Two Medium Onions (Chopped)
One Bell Pepper (Sliced)
Green Onions (Chopped)
Three Hard Boiled Eggs
Parmesan Cheese
Butter
Nutmeg
Pimento - Salt - Pepper

Steam the spinach for five minutes. Sauté the onion in olive oil and butter. Then add bell pepper and green onions until they are tender. Season with the spices and let it cook for another five minutes. Add the spinach, the eggs and parmesan cheese.

Make sure to keep the filo dough wrapped with a wet towel to keep it moist. Spray an oven dish with PAM and place 3 or 4 layers of filo. Add the filling and cover with another four layers of filo dough. Press the borders together and give it a twist. Beat an egg and using a brush cover the top. Bake at 250 degrees for about 20 minutes or until it looks golden. Let it cool before serving.

CREOLE STEAKS

INGREDIENTS

Two lbs. of Steaks (Cut in Thin Slices) (Replacement: Vegetarian Meat)
Six Potatoes Cut in Slices
Six Tomatoes Cut in Slices
Three Onions Cut in Thin Strips
Six Red Bell Peppers Cut in Round Slices
Olive Oil
Three Cups of Broth (Chicken Broth or Vegetable Broth)
Salt, Pepper, Paprika and Cumin

Season the beef with salt and pepper and place in a pot and pour some olive oil, on top of the meat add a layer of potatoes, then a layer of tomatoes, then a layer of onions and green bell pepper. Season well with salt and pepper and repeat one more time, all the layers, always pouring some olive oil. Cover with the broth and cook covered at low temperature for about 30 minutes or until the meat and vegetables are tender and well cooked.

MILANESAS

INGREDIENTS

One Lb. of Beef (Tender Beef in Slices)   (can replace with Veggie Patties)
One Cup of Crumbed Bread or more if needed
Three Minced Garlic Cloves
Parsley
Three Eggs
Salt, Oregano and Pepper
Olive Oil
Lemon Juice and/or Mayonnaise

Cut the meat in very thin slices and pound the meat if needed to make it more tender. In a bowl beat the eggs, with parsley, garlic, salt, oregano and pepper. Dip each slice into the egg mix, making sure it is all covered and smothered with the egg, and then dip it into a plate with bread crumbs, pressing down or punching a little to ensure the bread crumb covers each slice well. Fry in hot olive oil until it looks medium brown on both sides. Sprinkle with lemon juice and can also add mayonnaise on top.

Serve with mash potatoes and salad.

GUISO

INGREDIENTS

Two Cups of Tender Meat Cut in Cubes (Can Be Replaced by Vegetarian Meat)
One Big onion Cut in Slices
One Sweet Green Pepper (Minced)
One Can of Tomatoes
A couple of Bay leaves
Half Teaspoon of Cumin
Half Teaspoon of Paprika
One Can of Sweet Peas
Two Cups of Rice
Three Cups of Hot Water
Salt, Pepper and Parmesan Cheese
Half Cup of Olive Oil

Sautee the meat in a pan with the olive oil, add the minced onions, and green pepper and fry for a few minutes. Add the bay leaves, cumin, paprika and continue frying for a few more minutes. Add the rice, stirring to make sure that all ingredients are well mixed, add the tomato, salt and the hot water. Cover and let it cook at low temperature for about 15 minutes. Then add the sweet peas, and let it cook for two more minutes. Stop cooking, stir again with a spoon and let it rest for about five minutes.

Serve hot with lots of Parmesan cheese on top.

ESTOFADO

INGREDIENTS

Half a pound of Tender Meat (can use Tofu)
One Cup of Olive Oil
One Large Onion (Chopped)
Three Garlic Cloves (Crushed)
Three Whole Garlic Cloves Cut in Half
One Can of Tomato Sauce
One Can of tomato Paste
Sausage (Cut in pieces)
Dried Mushrooms (Place in Water for About One Hour)
One Cup of White Wine
Chicken or Vegetable Broth
Salt and Pepper

Make holes in the meat and fill it up with garlic clove halves. In a saucepan sauté the meat with the olive oil and then take it out. Add the onions and crushed garlic to the oil and sauté, add the meat and let it cook on low for 30 minutes. Add the rest of the ingredients and lower the temperature, and keep cooking for about 45 minutes. Cut the meat into slices before serving.

LENTILS

INGREDIENTS

One Pack of Lentils
Two Chopped Onions
Three Crushed Garlic Cloves
Two Carrots (Cut in Slices)
Sausage or Bacon (cut into Pieces) (Can Replace with Vegetarian Meat)
One Can of Tomato Sauce
Oregano
Paprika
Olive Oil
Chicken or Vegetable Broth
Salt

In a skillet sauté the onions with the garlic and parsley, add the carrots and the sausage, then the tomato and the lentils (Previously washed and soaked) add the seasonings. Lower the temperature and let it simmer for about 30 minutes or until the lentils are tender. Add broth as needed.

BAKED MEAT AND POTATOES

INGREDIENTS

One Lb. of Tenderloin (or Tofu)
Six White Potatoes
Six Sweet Potatoes
Four Carrots
Two Bell Pepper (Sliced)
Four Onions (Diced in thin layers)
Six Garlic Cloves (Chopped)
Three Fresh Tomatoes
Parsley
Oregano - Salt and Pepper
Olive Oil

Cut the meat, potatoes, carrots, bell pepper and tomatoes about the same size each. Mix all ingredients together and season well with olive oil, parsley, oregano, salt and pepper. Place all ingredients in a baking dish making sure they are covered with the oil and bake for about 45 at 350 degrees.

Keep an eye and add broth if needed to make sure all the ingredients are well cooked but not burnt.

CHICKEN A LA CREME

INGREDIENTS

One Whole Chicken
Two Onions
One Cup of Heavy Cream
Olive Oil
Salt and Pepper
White Wine

Wash the chicken and cut into pieces. Fry the onions, add the chicken and cook for 30 minutes. Add the cream, salt, pepper, and the wine and let it simmer for another 20 minutes. Serve with baked potatoes.

FILET MIGNON A LA CRÈME

INGREDIENTS

One Lb. or more of Filet Mignon (Cut in Pieces)
Two Onions (Chopped)
One Cup of Heavy Cream
Oil
Salt and Pepper
White Wine

Fry the the onions, add the meat and cook for 30 minutes. Add the cream, the salt, pepper, and the wine and let it simmer for another 40 minutes. Serve with baked potatoes or pasta.

SAFFRON RICE

INGREDIENTS

Two Sticks of Butter
One Onion
One Pack of White Rice
Chicken Broth (or Veggie Broth)
Three Cups of Warm Water
Saffron

Sautees the onion with one sticks of butter and add the rice, mixing with the wooden spoon to avoid sticking. When it looks golden, add the chicken broth and the saffron. Let it cook in low temperature for about 25 minutes. Once cooked, add the remaining butter and place in a dish cover with parmesan cheese.

MATAMBRE
(Stuffed Flank Steak)

INGREDIENTS

Two Lbs. of Flank Steak
Half a Cup of Red Wine Vinegar
One Teaspoon Finely Chopped Garlic
One Teaspoon Dried Thyme
Three Cups of Beef Stock
One to Three Cups of Cold Water

THE STUFFING

Half Lb. Fresh Spinach (Washed, Drained, and Trimmed of Stems)
Eight Cooked Carrots
Four Hard Boiled Eggs (Cut into Quarters)
One Large Onion (Sliced into Rings)
One Bunch of Fresh Parsley Finely Chopped
Ground Black Pepper
One Tablespoon of Coarse Salt

Cut the steaks by slicing them horizontally from one long side to the opposite side. Trim of all sinew and fat. Lay one steak in a pan and sprinkle with half the vinegar, half the garlic, and half the thyme. Cover with the other steak, and sprinkle with remaining vinegar, garlic, and thyme. Cover and marinate for six hours at room temperature, or overnight in the refrigerator. Lay the steaks end-to-end, in the direction of the grain of the meat, so that they overlap by about two inches.

~CONTINUED~

Pound the overlapping area to join them securely. Spread the spinach leaves evenly over the meat, and arrange the carrots across the grain of the meat in parallel rows about three inches apart. Place the egg quarters between the carrots. Scatter the onion rings over the meat, and sprinkle the surface with the parsley, salt and pepper. Carefully roll the matambre with the grain, into a thick, long cylinder. Tie at 1 inch intervals with a butcher string. Place the matambre in a large casserole or roasting pan along with the beef stock. Add enough cold water to come a third of the way up the roll. Cover tightly and bake at 375° for one hour. To serve, remove the matambre to a cutting board and let rest for 10 minutes. Remove strings and cut into 1/4 inch slices. Moisten with a little pan liquid, which can also be served on the side. Alternately, press the matambre under weights to until the juices drain off, refrigerate thoroughly, and slice before serving.

MEAT BALLS

INGREDIENTS

One Lb. of Ground Beef (Can use Veggie Ground Beef)
Bread (any kind you normally use; French or White sliced)
One cup and a half of Milk
Three Eggs (beaten)
Chopped Parsley
Crushed Garlic
Oregano
Salt and Pepper
Flour (only if needed)
Crumbed Bread
Olive Oil

In a bowl place bread cut into pieces and add the milk. Let it stand 10 minutes to soften. In another bowl beat the eggs, add the meat and the bread, add parsley, garlic, oregano, salt and pepper and work it for a minute to make sure it is all well mixed. Make small balls with your hands (If the meat is too soft you may want to add a little flour to be able to handle), and roll them over the crumbed bread and place them in the frying pan already hot with olive oil and fry them until they are dark brown.

CASTILLE CHICK-PEAS

INGREDIENTS

Two Cups of Chick-peas
Ham
Sausage (or Veggie Sausage)
Bacon (or Veggie Bacon)
Tow Onions (Chopped)
Two Garlic Cloves (Crushed)
Two Peeled Tomatoes
Olive Oil
Cayenne Pepper
Saffron
Chopped Parsley

Place the chickpeas in water all night (24 hours). Cut the ham, the sausage and bacon in small pieces and put it all with the chick-peas with enough water to cook for about 3 hours, or until the peas are soft. Sauté the onion in the olive oil, and add the garlic and the tomatoes. Add the cayenne pepper and saffron dissolved in water and the parsley. Add the chickpeas with the ham and sausage and let it cook for about 30 minutes.

POT AU FEU

INGREDIENTS

Three Beef Shanks with meat (Can Use Chicken, or Hen)
Half Lb. of Beef Marrow Bones
Bacon
Sausage
Four Potatoes (Cut in Half)
Four Sweet Potatoes (Cut in Half)
One Yellow Squash (Cut in Pieces)
One Cabbage
One Bunch of Spinach
Six Corns on the Cob
Chick-peas 1 can (fresh is better but need to be soaked in water overnight)
Garbanzo Beans 1 can (fresh need to be soaked in water overnight)
Basil Leaves
One Teaspoon of Thyme
Six Carrots (Cut in Pieces)
Three Leeks (Cut in Pieces)
Two Onions (Cut in Half)
Three Celeries (Cut in Pieces)
Salt and Pepper

Combine all ingredients in a very big crock pot with enough water to cover all ingredients, and cook on low 3 to 4 hours, or until all the ingredients are cooked and the meat very tender. You may need to add water. Taste and adjust seasonings.

Place the meats on a platter with the vegetables, season with olive oil and lemon, and serve with mustard on the side. Keep it warm. Strain the broth, and serve separately in cups.

This is the most typical Argentine dish!

CHIMICHURRI

This very Argentine sauce is especially for steaks on a grill. Great on char grilled, flank steak and any type of barbecue.

INGREDIENTS

One Bunch of Parsley
Minced garlic (about 8 cloves+-)
One Cup of Olive Oil
Half a Cup of Red Vinegar
Lemon Juice
One Tablespoon of Diced Red Onions
Oregano, Pepper and Salt

Chop the parsley in a food processor. Add the remaining ingredients and blend.

Use this sauce to cover your cooked meat.

RICE CAKES

INGREDIENTS

Two Cups and a Half of Cooked Rice
Three Eggs (Beaten)
Chopped Parsley
Crushed Garlic
Oregano
Salt and Pepper
One Cup of Flour
Olive Oil

In a bowl mix the cooked rice with the eggs, the parsley, garlic, oregano, salt and pepper and flour and form small balls shaped as cakes with your hands, adding more flour if needed. Fry in hot oil until they look golden brown.

SPINACH CAKES

INGREDIENTS

Two Cups and a Half of Cooked Spinach
Three Eggs (Beaten)
Chopped Parsley
Crushed Garlic
Oregano
Salt and Pepper
One Cup of Flour
Olive Oil

In a bowl mix the cooked spinach previously chopped, with the eggs, the parsley, garlic, oregano, salt and pepper and flour and form small balls shaped as cakes with your hands, adding more flour if needed. Fry in hot oil until they look golden brown.

POLENTA

INGREDIENTS

Two Cups of Yellow Corn meal
Two Chopped Onions
One Can of Tomato Sauce
One Cup and a Half of Chicken or Vegetable Broth
Crushed Garlic
Parsley
Salt and Pepper
Mozzarella Cheese
Parmesan Cheese

Sauté the onions with the garlic, and parsley. Then, add the tomato sauce, the broth and the yellow corn and let it cook for about ten minutes, stirring and watching over to make sure it does not burn, or get stuck at the bottom of the pan. Once cooked add the mozzarella and mix well. Pour into a dish and cover with Parmesan cheese. Serve hot.

PIO NONO

INGREDIENTS

Two Ounces of Flour
One Teaspoon of Starch
One Teaspoon of Honey
Six tablespoon of Sugar (=2.6 OZ)
Four Eggs
Vanilla

FILLING

Mayonnaise
Lettuce (Cut Small)
Tomato (Cut in Slices)
Swiss Cheese
Feta Cheese
Ham or any Meat of your choice (or Any Vegetarian Meat)
Hard Boil Eggs (Cut in Pieces)
Red Bell Peppers in Oil (Sliced)
Olives

Beat the eggs, first the white eggs, then add the yellow eggs, add the honey, the sugar until the preparation is thick and smooth. Add the starch, folding carefully, not to get air inside. Cover the oven dish with parchment paper and spray with butter, covering all the edges too then pour the mix.

Bake at 375 Degrees for approximate five minutes. After is baked turn it over a flat surface and take the paper out. Let it cool.

~CONTINUED~

Then spread the mayonnaise all over and cover with the filling ingredients, then wrap in a cylinder shape, and top with more mayonnaise and cover with olives.

To serve cut into slices.

LIVER AND ONIONS

INGREDIENTS

Liver (Cut in Slices)
Onions (Cut in Rings)
Crushed Garlic
Chopped Parsley
Oregano
Salt and Pepper
Olive Oil

Sauté the onions and add the liver. When liver starts to look cooked, add the rest of the ingredients. Let it cook for 20 minutes in low temperature. Serve hot with mash potatoes.

VITEL TONE

INGREDIENTS

Two Lbs. of Roast Beef
One Can of Tuna
Six Anchovies
One Cup of Mayonnaise
Vinegar
Half Cup of Olive Oil
Two Hard Boiled Eggs
Red Pepper in Oil (Cut in Slices)
Salt, Pepper and Mustard

Cook the roast beef in water with some vegetables for taste, and once cooked let it cool. Then cut into slices and place it on a dish.

In a bowl put the tuna, the anchovies and mix with a fork, then add the mayonnaise, the mustard, salt, oil and vinegar and mix well to form a paste. Cover the meat with this preparation and garnish on top with the hard boiled eggs and the red peppers.

RUSSIAN SALAD

INGREDIENTS

Cooked white potatoes cut into pieces
Cooked beets cut into pieces
One Can of Sweet Peas
Cook Carrots Cut into Pieces
Six Hard Boiled Eggs
One Cup of Mayonnaise
Salt and vinegar

In a salad bowl mix all ingredients, add salt and vinegar to taste and then mayonnaise. Let it cool in the fridge before serving.

SPANISH TORTILLA

INGREDIENTS

Potatoes
One Big Onion (Sliced and Sauté)
One Red Bell Pepper (Sliced)
Sausage (can use Veggie Sausage)
Two Eggs
Three Teaspoons of Milk
Olive Oil
Salt and Pepper

Peel and cut the potatoes in small pieces and fry them, then fry the onions separately. Let it cool. In a bowl mix the potatoes and the onions. Beat the eggs with the milk and add to the potatoes, then add the remaining ingredients and seasoning. Pour the mix into a hot frying pan cook at low temperature. Turn the tortilla on the other side to cook both sides, making sure it does not break.

EGGS IN WHITE SAUCE

INGREDIENTS

One Cup of Milk
One Teaspoon of Corn Starch
Half Stick of Butter
Half Teaspoon of Nutmeg
Salt and Pepper
Six Hard Boiled Eggs
Crumbed Bread
Olive Oil

Boil 6 eggs for about 20 minutes, and when they are cooked let them cool. Prepare the white sauce with the milk, butter, nutmeg, corn starch dissolved in cool water, salt and pepper. Boil the milk and let it cook at slow temperature until the sauce gets thick. Let it cool.

Cut the eggs in half and place them in the white sauce, then pass the eggs for crumbed bread and form a ball. Fry them in hot oil.

CHICKEN A LA SALTENA

INGREDIENTS

One Whole Clean Chicken Cut into Pieces
Two Sticks of Butter
One Medium Onion (Cut into Slices)
Basil Leaves - Salt and pepper
1/3 Cup of Port Wine - 1/3 Cup of Gin -
1/3 Cup of Cognac - 1/3 Cup of Ron
1 Cup of Milk
Two Ounces of Butter
Two Spoonful of Flour
A pinch of Nutmeg
Two Beaten Yellow Eggs

In a saucepan melt the butter and add the chicken, and cook until the chicken is golden. Then add the onions, basil leaves, salt and fresh pepper. Cover and let it cook for 20 minutes a medium temperature. Then add all the liquors, the nutmeg and continue cooking uncovered for 10 more minutes. Once cooked cover and keep it warm.

Mix the milk (saving 1/3 cup of milk) with the butter and bring it to boil. Mix the 1/3 cup of milk with a little flour and add to the previous milk, stirring constantly, then add the yellow eggs.

Put the chicken in a dish and cover with the cream.

OSSOBUCO

INGREDIENTS

Four Shanks with meat
Flour
Three Tablespoon of Olive Oil
A Quart of a Cup of White Wine
Half a Cup of Broth
Medium Onion (Cut into Slices)
One Carrot (Cut into Pieces)
One Leek (Chopped)
One Celery (Cut into Small Pieces)
Cloves
One Can of Tomato Paste
Lemon Peel
One Garlic Clove
Salt and Pepper

Season the meat with flour, salt and pepper, and sauté with the olive oil until the meat is cooked on both sides. Take it out of the frying sauce and place the meat in a larger sauce pan. Leave the oil in the frying pan. Add the wine, the broth, and a few cloves. When it starts boiling lower the temperature and let it simmer for ten minutes.

Meanwhile, heat the oil left in the frying pan and add the onions, the carrots, the leak and sauté for 5 minutes. Add this to the meat add also the lemon peel, the tomato paste, salt and pepper.

Cover and let it cook at low temperature for about 1 ½ hour.

PESTO SAUCE

INGREDIENTS

Basil Leaves
Six Cloves of Garlic
Half a Cup of Pecan or Walnuts
Half Cup of Olive Oil
Salt

Clean all ingredients and put them in a chopper, when you have a mix add the oil and salt to taste. Mix well and pour into a glass container. Use this sauce on fresh pasta with Parmesan cheese on top.

RICOTTA CHEESE PIE

DOUGH INGREDIENTS

Half a Cup of Butter
One Cup of Sugar
Three Eggs
One Quart Cup of Milk
Vanilla Extract
Two Ounces and six of Flour

Mix all the ingredients together, and knead with both hands until the dough is smooth. Cut in two pieces and with a rolling pin stretch the dough and place it in a buttered pie dish. Leave the second part for the top.

FILLING INGREDIENTS

Half Cup of Ricotta Cheese
One Egg
One Teaspoon of Grated Lemon Peel (or Orange)
One Cup and a Half of Sugar

Mix all the ingredients in a bowl with a mixer.

Pour the mix into the pie dish and cover with the second dough. Brush the top of the pie with a yellow egg, and bake for about 35 minutes at 375 degrees.

CHURROS WITH HOT CHOCOLATE

INGREDIENTS

Half Cup of Water
A Pinch of salt
One Cup and a Half of Flour
Oil
Sugar

Boil water and add the flour and salt, and cook until it is a paste and it comes out of the saucepan easily.

Put the mix in a churrera and pour abut 7 inches long churros into a frying pan with hot oil. Fry it for about 3 minutes or until it turns dark yellow. Place it in a dish and cover with sugar.

Hot Chocolate

Boil milk with one cooking chocolate bar per cup, add a teaspoon of starch, dissolved in a little bit of cold water, sugar, and cook for one more minute. Serve hot with churros.

CROISSANTS

INGREDIENTS

300 Grams of Flour
One Envelope of Yeast
1/4 Cup of Warm water
One Cup of Sugar
A pinch of Salt
3.5 Ounces of Butter
One Eggs
One Beaten Egg

Dissolve the yeast in lukewarm water and add the flour, making a ball. Immerse in a bowl of water until it floats.

Add the rest of the flour in a crown shape on the table and put the butter, salt and the sugar in the center. Work the dough with your hands and add the eggs one by one. Add the yeast and keep working the dough. Leave the dough in a bowl for about half an hour or until double its volume. Keep it in the refrigerator until it cools down.

Then, put the dough on the table and sprinkle with flour and spread until it becomes very thin. Cut in triangle shape pieces. Roll these pieces giving them the shape of croissants.

Place the croissant on a buttered pan and leave them until they raise twice their size. Brush all over with the beaten egg, and bake for about 25 to 30 minutes.

~CONTINUED~

Serve the croissants with Milk Jelly on top.

Milk Jelly

Place one opened can of condensed milk in an open container with hot water and let the water boil for approximate 20 minutes, or until the milk turns dark brown. Let it cool down. Cover the croissants with a spoon of Jelly.

SWEET EMPANADAS

Use the dough that we used for "Meat Empanadas" as indicated earlier but fill each with "Dulce de Batata" or "Dulce de Membrillo" cut into pieces—You can find these dulces in any Latin store.

You can fry or baked as you prefer.

DRUNKEN PIE

INGREDIENTS

Lady Fingers (the best are "Vainillas" at any Latin store)these are crunchier and sweeter!
Brandy, Vermouth, or Port Wine
1. Yellow Cream
2. Butter Cream
3. Chantilly Cream
Prepare the creams first.

YELLOW CREAM
Two Cups of Milk
Three Eggs
One Cup and a Half of Sugar
One Teaspoon of Starch
Vanilla Extract

In a sauce-pan put the milk, the sugar, the eggs and mix them well, and then add the starch dissolved in bit of cold water, and cook at slow temperature, stirring constantly for about 5 minutes. When it is done, add the vanilla extract, and let it cool.

BUTTER CREAM
Sweet Butter
Sugar
Vanilla Extract
Blend the butter with sugar and Vanilla.

~CONTINUED~

CHANTILLY CREAM
Twp Cups of Heavy Cream
One Cup and a half of Confectionery Sugar
One or Two Teaspoons of Vanilla Extract

In a bowl beat the heavy cream with an electric mixer, with the sugar and the vanilla until it get thick. Keep it cool!

Once you have all creams done, place the lady fingers in a large dish and pour some brandy, vermouth, or port wine, over the lady fingers to make them wet, now add the Yellow cream. Put another layer of lady fingers, and pour more brandy and now the butter cream. Finally, put another layer of lady fingers and pour more brandy and cover with the Chantilly cream. Place in the refrigerator for at least 30 minutes before serving.

ENGLISH SOUP

INGREDIENTS

BASIC CAKE

Ten Yellow Eggs
Eight White Eggs (Beaten)
8.8 Ounces of Sugar
7.5 Ounces of Flour
Lemon Peel
5.3 Ounces of Butter

YELLOW CREAM

Two Cups of Milk
Three Eggs
One Cup and a Half of Sugar
Half a Cup of Flour
Vanilla
Quarter of a Cup of Cognac

CHANTILLY CREAM

Two Cups of Heavy Cream
One Cup and a Half of Confectionery Sugar
One teaspoon of Vanilla Extract

~CONTINUED~

CARAMEL

Two Cups of Sugar
One Cup of water
Cognac
Chopped Pecans

First make the basic cake: In a bowl beat the white eggs with the sugar until they are thick. Add the yellow eggs, the butter, the vanilla and the lemon and fold everything together and bake at 350 degrees for about 30 minutes approximately.

Then make the yellow Cream: In a sauce-pan put the sugar, the four, the eggs and mix them well at slow temperature, stirring constantly for about five minutes. When it is done, add the vanilla extract and cognac, and let it cool.

Make the Chantilly Cream:
In a bowl beat the heavy cream with an electric mixer, with the sugar and the vanilla extract until it gets thick.

Prepare the Caramel: (Last Step)
In a saucepan put the sugar and add the water and cook at slow temperature for about 10 minutes or until it turns an amber color. Use immediately.

Once, you have all the elements ready, cut the cake in four layers. Add the caramel and cognac to all these layers first. Then place one layer and cover with the yellow cream and the next layer and repeat until you have the four layers back together. Then cover with the Chantilly cream and sprinkle with the pecans on top.

BREAD PUDDING

INGREDIENTS

Three Cups of Bread (Cut into Small Pieces)
One Cup of Flour
One Cup and a Half of Milk
Two sticks of Butter
Two Cups of Sugar
One or two Teaspoons of Vanilla Extract
Six Eggs
One Cup and a Half of Seedless Raisins
Half Cup of Crushed Pecans

In a bowl put the bread and add the milk and let it soak for about 15 minutes. Beat the white eggs and add sugar and keep beating until it gets thick, add the white eggs to the bread, add the yellow eggs, the butter, the rest of the sugar, the vanilla, the flour, and mix all together folding it, then add the raisins and the pecans. Bake in a pudding pan previously greased, at 350 degrees for about 1 1/2 hour. Insert a knife to see when it is done. The knife should come a little bit moist but not wet. Let it cool.

ENGLISH PUDDING

INGREDIENTS

Three Quarters of a Cup of Butter
One Cup of Sugar
Six Eggs
One Cup of Flour
Half a Spoonful of Baking Powder
Three Spoonful of Candied Fruits (if you like them)
Four Spoonful of Seedless Raisins (soaked in Ron and passed in flour)
Vanilla Extract

In a bowl mix the butter with the sugar until it smooth and add the eggs one by one, then the flour, the baking powder, the fruits and raisins, and the Vanilla, very slowly until is well mixed. Then pour the mix into a greased pan and bake in the oven at 350 degrees for about 30 minutes.

PANCAKES

INGREDIENTS

Three Cups of Flour
Four Eggs
One Cup of Milk
Half a Stick of Butter
Vanilla Extract

In a blender mix all ingredients together until you have a smooth cream. In a greased and hot fry pan pour a little of the mix and move the pan around to spread the cream completely, turning the pancake around to cook on both sides. The pancakes should be thin! Place it on a dish and cook the next one. After you have made about 10 pancakes, fill each of them with Milk Jelly and roll them and sprinkle with sugar.

BUÑUELOS

INGREDIENTS

Three Cups of Flour
Four Eggs
One Cup of Milk
Half a Stick of Butter
Vanilla Extract

Bananas cut into pieces

Put all ingredients in a bowl and mix well then add the bananas and with a spoon pick each banana piece with plenty of mix and fry in hot oil until it looks golden brown. Place on a dish and sprinkle with sugar.

You can use "Dulce de Batata" instead of Bananas. Which you can find at any Latin Store.

COCONUT FLAN

INGREDIENTS

One Cup of Sugar
One Third Cup of Water
Four Eggs
One Can of Condensed Milk
One Pot of Whipping Cream (medium)
One can of Grated Coconut

In a small saucepan heat the sugar and the water without mixing. Cook slow for about 10 minutes or until the caramel looks amber. Spread the caramel evenly in an oven-dish.

Beat the white eggs until the eggs get thick, then add the yellow eggs, the condensed milk, whipping cream, grated coconut. Fold the cream to mix very smoothly. Place the baking dish in a bigger dish with water and bake in the oven at 325 degrees for about forty minutes to one hour. Let it cool before serving.

RUSSIAN IMPERIAL

INGREDIENTS

Eight White eggs
Two Cups of Sugar
Quarter of a Cup of Crushed almonds
Cinnamon
Confectionery Sugar

CREAM

Two Sticks of Butter
One Cup and a Half of Sugar
One Spoon and a Half of Orange Juice
Half a Cup of Crushed Almonds
One Teaspoon of Almond Extract
Two Yellow Eggs

Beat the white eggs until they are smooth and thick and then add the sugar. Utilizing a decorating syringe with a flat tube make three squares and bake them at 250 degrees or until they are dried. Take them out and let them cool.

Cream: In a bowl mix the butter with the yellow eggs until is very creamy and cook at slow temperature. Then add the almonds, and the remaining ingredients very slowly until it is all well mixed. Let it cool.

Now, put a square and cover with this cream until you form a tower with all the flat squares and the cream. Cover all over with the cream and then sprinkle with confectionary sugar and cinnamon.

DULCE DE LECHE FLAN

INGREDIENTS

One Cup and a Half of Sugar
One Cup of Dulce de Leche
Two Cups and a Quart of Milk
Three Spoonful of Sugar
Four Yellow Eggs
One Egg
Vanilla Extract

In a saucepan put the sugar with a little water. Let it cook without mixing, slow until the caramel is golden. Pour the caramel into a baking pan and make sure that covers the whole pan, let it cool.

Boil the milk and add the spoons of sugar and mix, let it cool down. Beat the yellow eggs and add the whole egg and the dulce de leche, mixing well, then add the vanilla and the milk. Pour into the baking pan and bake in the oven, by placing the baking pan into another pan with water to cover three fourth of the pan. Cook for about 45 minutes at 350 degrees. Let it cool and then turn upside down to show the caramel on top. Keep in the refrigerator before serving.

PLAIN CONFECTION

INGREDIENTS

Six Eggs
One Cup of Sugar
Beaten Butter
Twp Teaspoons of Baking Powder
One Cup of Flour
One Teaspoon of Vanilla Extract

With an electric mixer beat the eggs. Add the vanilla extract and the butter. Mix the flour and the baking powder and add slowly to the mix, folding carefully. Grease a pan with butter and add the mix and bake at 350 degrees for about 30 minutes. Let it cool before taking it out of the pan.

MERENGUE DISCS

INGREDIENTS

Four White Eggs
Two Cups of Sugar

Place the white eggs in a bowl with a spoonful of sugar. Beat the eggs with an electric beater until the cream is thick. Add 1 cup of sugar and keep beating for ten minutes. Add the remaining sugar slowly. Place the meringue in a syringe and pour to form a disc on a dish covered with parchment paper. Make 2 discs and place in the center of the oven at very low temperature. The meringue should get dried not cooked or golden. You may want to leave the oven door open a little bit. Takes about two hours. This discs are ready to use the next day.

DULCE DE LECHE

INGREDIENTS

Three Liters of Milk (About four quarts of a gallon)
Two Lbs. of Sugar
Half a Teaspoon of Baking Powder
One Stick of Vanilla

Cook the milk with the sugar at slow temperature. When it starts boiling add the vanilla and the baking powder dissolved in cold milk. Lower the temperature and let it cook, stirring constantly until it get thick. Take with a spoon a little bit and put it on a plate, let it cool, if it is done it will be thick and it will not run. Take it out of the stove and place the pan in cold water, stirring constantly until it gets cool. Place in a jar and keep it in the refrigerator.

SWEET POTATO JAM

INGREDIENTS

Tem Small Sweet Potatoes
One Cup and a Half of Sugar
Cloves
Water

Wash the sweet potatoes and peel and let them soak in water for an hour. If the potatoes are big cut in half or small pieces. Take them out of the water and weight the potatoes. For each pound of potatoes you will need a little more than half a pound of sugar.

Boil the water with the sugar and the clove. When the water is boiling add the potatoes, and let it simmer. You will know is ready when the potato looks yellow translucent, and is soft and the water is turned into a thick syrup.

If you wish to bottle into jars, to keep it for a long time, you need to let it cool and then fill the jars (these are specialty jars with tight caps). After you filled these jars, place them in a pan with water and cover completely. Place on the stove and let it boil for about 8 minutes. Then, take them out and let them cool carefully, not getting any air vent that may crush the glass.

YELLOW SQUASH MARMALADE

INGREDIENTS

Four and a Half of Yellow Squash
Four and a Half of Sugar
Two Cups of Water
Two Cloves

Place in a big pan the squash cut into cubes with the sugar and cloves. Let it cook until the squash is tender. Smash the squash making a paste and continue cooking until it has almost no liquid. Get the cloves out and pour into the jar. Let it cool.

WINE LIQUOR

INGREDIENTS

Two Cups of Wine
Half a Cup of Ethyl Alcohol
One Stick of Cinnamon
Two Cups of Water
A Quart Cup of Sugar
Two and a Half Cups of Sugar

Place the wine, alcohol, cinnamon and the quarter cup of sugar in a glass container and stirring once a day to make sure the sugar gets dissolved, for 10 days and then filter. Place the sugar and water in a pot and cook until it makes a syrup, then add the mix and cook at slow temperature until it gets thick. Let it cook and pour into a bottle.

RICE PUDDING

INGREDIENTES

One Cup of Rice
Six Cups of Milk
One Cup of Sugar
Two Yellow Eggs
Grated Orange Peel
Cinnamon

Place the rice with the milk and let it soak for 4 hours. Then, add half a cup of sugar and cook at slow temperature for 12 minutes.

Beat the yellow eggs with half cup of sugar. Add slowly this mix to the hot milk and let it cook for two more minutes, stirring constantly. When the rice is cooked and thick and creamy, take it off, and let it cool.

Place in a dish and sprinkle with cinnamon.

PASTRY CREAM

INGREDIENTS

Two Cups of Milk
Four Spoonful of Sugar
Two Yellow Eggs
Two Spoonfuls of Sugar
Two Spoonfuls of Starch
One Spoonful of Butter
One or Two teaspoons of Vanilla Extract

Cook the milk with the two spoonfuls of sugar. In a bowl beat the yellow eggs with the other two spoonfuls of sugar. Dissolve the starch with a little bit of cold water or milk and add the eggs and the starch to the boiling milk, stirring constantly. Take it out of the stove and add the butter and the vanilla extract.

DELICATE STARCH CAKE

INGREDIENTS

Twp Sticks of Butter
One Cup and a Half of Sugar
Three Eggs
Half a Cup of Flour
Two Cups of Starch
Two Teaspoons of Baking Powder
One Quart of a Cup of Milk

Beat the butter with the sugar in a bowl until you make a cream. Beat the eggs in another bowl until they make a foam and add slowly to the cream, stirring all the time. In another bowl mix the flour with the starch and the baking powder and add to the mixture along with the milk, little of both at a time.

When all the ingredients are well mixed, pour this mix into a baking pan previously greased with plenty of butter and bake at 300 degrees for 45 minutes.

Let it cool and then place in a cake dish and sprinkle with confectionary sugar.

ALFAJORES

INGREDIENTS

Half a Cup of Butter approx. Five ounces (at room temperature)
Two Yellow Eggs
One Whole Egg
One Small Glass of Cognac
Vanilla Extract
Half a Teaspoon of Grated Lemon Peel
Sixteen Spoonful of Corn Starch
Ten Spoonful of Flour
One Teaspoon of Baking Powder

FILLING
Milk Jelly
Grated Coconut
Confectionary sugar or Chocolate

In a bowl beat the butter with the sugar until you make a cream, add the yellow eggs, and the whole egg, the cognac, the vanilla extract and the lemon peel. In another bowl mix the starch with the flour and the baking powder and add slowly to the mix, until you have a ball. On a surface covered with flour work the dough and then cover with a plastic film and let it rest in the refrigerator for thirty minutes.

Pre-heat the oven at approximate 325 degrees.

~CONTINUED~

83

On a floured surface place the ball and cut in two pieces. Spread the dough until you have a half inch thick dough and cut into medallions, the size you like, but remember that they will increase in size once baked.

Bake for 10 to 15 minutes until they are cooked but not golden. Let them cool, and then spread the milk jelly in the center of the medallion and cover with the other half. Sprinkle the alfajores with coconut.

You can cover with melted chocolate or confectionary sugar. I like to mix some with chocolate and some with sugar.

ALFAJORES MAR DEL PLATA STYLE

INGREDIENTS

One Cup and a Quart of Flour
Three Bars of Baking Chocolate
One Teaspoon of Baking Soda
Melted Butter
Confectionary Sugar
Vanilla Extract
Three Yellow Eggs
Flour
Butter

FILLING

Milk Jelly
Grated Baking Chocolate

Pre-heat the oven and put the flour in a baking sheet and into the oven with the door open, to let it dry, stirring with a spoon. When it gets a golden color, take it out and mix with the grated chocolate and the baking soda. Place on the table and form a well. In the center pour the melted butter, the sugar, the vanilla and the yellow eggs. Mix all ingredients, bringing the flour from the sides into the center. Knead the dough until you have a smooth dough and then with a rolling pin, spread the dough until it is half an inch thick. Cut medallions and place them on a baking sheet previously greased and bake for about 10 to 15 minutes.

~CONTINUED~

Let them cool, and then put a spoonful of milk jelly in the center and place another medallion on top and push to make the jelly spread. In a small saucepan heat the grated chocolate with water and when it is hot not boiling, place this saucepan into a larger one with water and let it cook at low temperature, stirring constantly until the chocolate is melted and creamy.

Use this chocolate to cover the alfajores on both sides.

Valuable Resources
for Vegetarian

Food Harvest Direct, Inc.
P.O. Box 988
Knoxville, TN 37901-0988
Tel.: 1-800-835-2867

Lumen Foods
409 Scott St.
Lake Charles, LA 70601
Tel.: 1-800-256-2253
www.soybean.com
Variety of fake meats.

Mail Order Catalog
P.O. Box 180
Summertown, TN 38483
Tel.: 1-800-695-2241
www.healthy-eating.com
Textured vegetable protein, nutritional yeast, instant gluten flour, and soy milk powder.

May Wah Healthy
Vegetarian Food, Inc.
213 Hester St. New York, NY 10013
Tel.: 212-334-4428
Fax: 212-334-4423
www.vegieworld.com
Delicious vegan faux fish and other faux meats.

Pangea
7829 Woodmont Ave. Bethesda, MD 20814
Tel.: 301-652-3181
www.VeganStore.com
Vegan chocolate, gelatin, cookies, cheese and more.

Worthington Foods
900 Proprietors Rd. Worthington, OH 43085
Tel.: 1-800-243-1810
Variety of faux meat products, including fake tuna ("Tuno"), a PETA favorite.
www.HappyCow.net
Provides a worldwide listing of
vegetarian restaurants

www.NoMeat.com
Provides online ordering of
vegan substitutes for meat,
dairy products, and eggs.

More useful Links:
http://www.peta.org/about/contact.asp
http://www.vegcooking.com/gb_intro.asp
http://www.bocaburger.com/main.aspx?m=meatless_burgers
http://www.yvesveggie.com/splash.php?referer=products_details.php&refererQS=product_id%3D9%26page%3D1%26pIdName%3DVeggie%2520Dogs
http://www.yvesveggie.comsplash.php?referer=products_family.php&refererQS=family_id%3D13%26page%3D1%26pIdName%3DDeli%2520Slices

Printed in the United States
72371LV00003B/160-165

9 781424 166299